# Why God Gave Us Friends

Written by Barbara Burrow

Illustrated by Asterio Pascolini

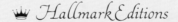

♛ Hallmark Editions

# Why God Gave Us Friends

God made the world with its towering trees, its mighty oceans and tranquil beaches.

He fashioned the majestic mountains,
the cool, green valleys and the quiet woodlands.

*He set the moon into its orbit*

　　　　*and placed the stars in the heavens.*

*He divided Time into seasons,*

*each with its own magnificent beauty.*

*He gave us dominion over the earth*

*and everything thereon…*

and all these things He gave us
for our benefit and pleasure.

Then in His great wisdom,
God looked down the corridors of Time
and foresaw the special needs of human hearts.

*He saw how often we would need*

*someone to share our inner thoughts and motives...*

someone who hears

        not merely the words we speak,

but our deeper feelings, for which there are no words…

*someone who knows the worth of silence*
*and listens without judging.*

That's why God gave us friends.

*He saw that we would sometimes need relief*

*from the frantic pace of competitive living...*

someone with whom we can drop all pretense,

who will love us,

not for what we may one day become,

but for what we are right now...

someone who will close his eyes to our human frailties
and see only that which is good in us.

*He knew our hearts would sometimes be burdened with sorrow and disappointment...*

and that we would need
someone who knows just when to speak
and when to stand silently by,
giving us strength and comfort by simply being near.

*That's why God gave us friends.*

*He saw that there would be times*

    *when we would become tired and discouraged…*

*and would need someone to encourage us*

*to reach our highest potential…*

*someone to cheer us on and bring us face-to-face*

*with our better selves.*

*He saw that there would be times*

*when we would stumble and fall...*

and would need someone to help us

pick ourselves up and try again...

someone who would teach us

to laugh at our mistakes

and help us find the rainbow after the rain.

*That's why God gave us friends.*

*God saw that we would sometimes*

*have to take a lonely stand*

*because of our convictions...*

and we would need

someone to support us when we're pursuing a dream...

*someone to humor us when we're impractical*

*and to stand beside us when we champion a cause.*

He knew our hearts would sometimes burst with joy
that must be shared to be fully experienced...

and that we would need

someone to praise us for our accomplishments

and rejoice with us in our good fortune...

*someone to increase our awareness*

*of the beautiful in life.*

*He foresaw our strengths, our weaknesses,*

*our dreams and our longings.*

*And so God gave us friends,*

*that we on earth might have a glimpse*

*of the joy of heaven…*